D1594913

RR

TCM 2668

Dr. Fry's
Homophones Workbook
Grades 3-6

by Edward Fry, Ph.D.
&
Margaret Langer, Ed.D

Teacher Created Materials, Inc.

BOWLING GREEN STATE UNIVERSITY
DISCARDED
LIBRARY

BOWLING GREEN STATE
UNIVERSITY LIBRARIES

Homophones Workbook

Grades 3–6

by Margaret Langer, Ed .D.
Department of Education
University of the Pacific
&
by Edward Fry, Ph.D.
Professor Emeritus
Rutgers University

Teacher Created Materials, Inc.
6421 Industry Way
Westminster, CA 92683

www.teachercreated.com

ISBN-1-57690-668-X

©1997 by Edward Fry
Laguna Beach Educational Books

©2000 Revised by Teacher Created Materials, Inc.
Reprinted, 2001
Made in U.S.A.

The classroom teacher may reproduce copies of materials in this book for classroom use only. The reproduction of any part for an entire school or school system is strictly prohibited. No part of this publication may be transmitted, stored, or recorded in any form without written permission from the publisher.

Table of Contents

Table of Contents *(cont.)*

Lessons *(cont.)*

Introduction

Computer spell checkers do not know the difference between *to* and *two* or the difference between *bear* and *bare,* but some writers don't know those differences either. Their mistakes are sometimes funny and sometimes embarrassing.

Homophones Workbook is designed to help writers learn that the English language sometimes has two or three different spellings of words which sound the same but have totally different meanings.

Words that sound the same but have different meanings and different spellings are called *homophones.* (Note: *Homonyms* are words that have the same sound and often the same spelling but have different meanings.) Homophones are particularly important to study as spelling words now that so many people use spell check programs on word processors. While spell check programs can catch many errors, these programs cannot notice a word spelled incorrectly if a homophone was used.

Each lesson in this workbook presents a set of homophones. Following the definitions and examples of the different spellings and meanings, a set of 10 fill-in-the-blank sentences is provided so students can practice using the right homophone in sentences. Because homophones are the basis for many jokes, riddles, and puns, they have been included as a "Challenge." Students are also asked to create their own sentences or jokes using the homophones.

When learning to spell words, there is a "5-Step Spelling Word Study Method for Students," which is particularly useful. That method consists of the following steps:

1. **Look** at the whole word carefully.
2. **Say** the word aloud to yourself.
3. **Spell** the word. Say each letter to yourself.
4. **Write** the word from memory. Cover the word and write it.
5. **Check** your written word against the correct spelling. Circle errors, and repeat steps 4 and 5.

Students should be taught to use three additional strategies when studying homophones. First, visual memory techniques should be emphasized. This means closing one's eyes and trying to "see the word" in one's mind. Second, there needs to be an emphasis on connecting the right spelling with the right meaning. Using short key phrases, such as "a lion's tail" versus "a story tale" may be helpful. Finally, memory devices (mnemonics) can also help students to remember the difference, such as *hear* has an *ear* in it, which is used for listening; the other *here* refers to a place, and the spelling is close to *there.*

For English as a Second Language (ESL) students, homophones are one of the great mysteries of the English language. For native English speakers, homophones are a troublesome yet important part of learning to read and write. This workbook will be helpful for students in grades three through six, for remedial students, and for students for whom English is a second language.

Note: We suggest you have a spelling test after every 10 lessons.

ant   aunt

An **ant** is a small insect that gets into food and usually lives underground.

Your **aunt** is a woman who is your mother's or father's sister.

    Example: My **aunt** saw an **ant** on the cake.

Fill in each of these sentences with the correct **ant** or **aunt**.

1. There is an _____ in the sugar bowl.

2. My brother has _____s in his pants.

3. My _____ is coming to visit us.

4. I have an _____ who lives far away.

5. An _____ has six legs.

6. My friend gets presents from two _____s.

7. Does your _____ live near here?

8. There must be a hundred _____s in that hill.

9. Please get the _____ off that food.

10. My _____ has no children of her own.

Challenge: What do you call an ant's father's sister? *(An aunt ant.)*

Practice: Write a sentence or a joke using each of the above homophones.

_____

_____

already   all ready

The word **already** means earlier or previously.

The words **all ready** means completely prepared.

Example: She was **all ready** to go, but her friends had **already** left.

Fill in each of these sentences with the correct **already** or **all ready**.

1. The group was _____ to go on the trip.

2. I was _____ tired after the long walk.

3. The bus was supposed to be here _____.

4. The army was _____ for the war to begin.

5. The bill _____ was paid.

6. The potatoes were _____ for cooking.

7. Mother _____ went shopping.

8. Are you _____ for school to begin?

9. My school work is _____ done.

10. We are _____ for the party to start.

Challenge: What could you say if things were prepared and just waiting to go? *(All's ready already.)*

Practice: Write a sentence or a joke using each of the above homophones.

_____

_____

eight   ate

The word **eight** is a number that is one more than seven.

The word **ate** is the past tense of the verb eat, meaning to have consumed food.

   Example: I felt sick after I **ate** those **eight** candy bars.

Fill in each of these sentences with the correct **eight** or **ate**.

   1. If you take one from nine, you get _____.

   2. There are _____ flies on my sandwich.

   3. Who _____ my sandwich?

   4. You burp because of something you _____.

   5. _____ people in a car is too many.

   6. I _____ too much last night.

   7. I _____ two eggs this morning.

   8. There are _____ people at the table.

   9. Four and four make _____.

   10. Who _____ the last cookie?

Challenge: What number is never hungry? *(Eight.)*

Practice: Write a sentence or a joke using each of the above homophones.

_____

_____

eye   I

An **eye** is the part of the body through which a person sees.

The word **I** is a pronoun which refers to the person speaking or writing.

Example: **I** covered one **eye** with my hand.

Fill in each of these sentences with the correct **eye** or **I**.

1. Please don't hit me in the _____.

2. If you are good, _____ will be good to you.

3. Be careful when you say, "_____ love you."

4. His right _____ was closed.

5. Use a telescope with only one _____.

6. _____ need to go home now.

7. Most animals have two _____s.

8. May _____ go with you?

9. How did you get that black _____?

10. _____ ran into a door.

Challenge: What did one eye say to the other? *(Between you and me, something smells.)*

Practice: Write a sentence or a joke using each of the above homophones.

_____

_____

bare   bear

Bare means uncovered. It also can mean empty or plain.

A **bear** is a large, furry animal that eats honey. It also means to carry something or to have a child.

      Example: The ice chest was **bare** because a **bear** got into it.

Fill in each of these sentences with the correct **bare** or **bear**.

  1. The hunter shot a _____.

  2. If you wear no shoes, you are _____footed.

  3. That football player is as big as a _____.

  4. In a bathing suit you are mostly _____.

  5. A room with no furniture looks _____.

  6. If the load is too heavy, you can't _____ it.

  7. The top of the hill was _____.

  8. He wore no hat; his head was _____.

  9. Our cat will soon _____ kittens.

10. It takes two men to _____ that stone.

Challenge: What is a large animal without a fur coat? *(A bare bear.)*

Practice: Write a sentence or a joke using each of the above homophones.

_____

_____

ball   bawl

A **ball** is a rounded object used in sports and games. It is also a formal gathering for a dance.

To **bawl** means to cry loudly or shout out at the top of one's voice.

Example: The little boy started to **bawl** when he got hit by the **ball**.

Fill in each of these sentences with the correct **ball** or **bawl**.

1. Don't throw that _____ at my head.

2. I could hear that baby _____ a block away.

3. Every fall I watch foot_____ games.

4. He _____ed me out for breaking his bike.

5. The _____ game was a waste of time.

6. When he was unhappy, he would _____.

7. The lost cat _____ed for its mother.

8. I got a new soccer _____ for my birthday.

9. Most _____s are round.

10. I don't like to hear someone _____ing.

Challenge: Why was Cinderella thrown off the baseball team? *(Because she ran away from the ball.)*

Practice: Write a sentence or a joke using each of the above homophones.

_____

_____

sell   cell

Sell means to exchange something for money.

A **cell** is a small space or room, like a jail cell. It can also refer to the smallest unit of an organism, like a one-cell animal. Cell is also the abbreviation for a cellular phone.

Example: Can I **sell** you this **cell**?

Fill in each of these sentences with the correct **sell** or **cell**.

1. You can _____ lots of ice cream on hot days.

2. Don't _____ all of your clothes.

3. You might not like to live in a jail _____.

4. Your body is made up of lots of tiny _____s.

5. If you don't like it, maybe you can _____ it.

6. The bee _____s were full of honey.

7. The man tried to _____ me his car.

8. Do you want to _____ your house?

9. Call me on my _____ phone.

10. A _____ is a very small room.

Challenge: Why couldn't the prisoner make any money? *(Because he was selling from a cell.)*

Practice: Write a sentence or a joke using each of the above homophones.

_____

_____

to   two   too

To is a word that generally means in the direction of. Sometimes it is also used before a verb as in "to eat."

Two is a number that is one less than three.

Too means also.

Example: I went **to** the store, **too**, but only bought **two** things.

Fill in each of these sentences with the correct **to**, **two**, or **too**.

1. John has _____ computers.

2. Please do not laugh at me, _____.

3. I would love _____ go on a long walk.

4. Today _____ dollars won't buy much.

5. Their family has some problems, _____.

6. I want it _____ happen soon.

7. I have _____ feet.

8. When can we go _____ the show?

9. Don't eat _____ much food.

10. Let's go _____ the game later.

Challenge: What did the twins wear to their dance recital? *(Two tutus.)*

Practice: Write a sentence or a joke using each of the above homophones.

LESSON 9

bee   be

A **bee** is an insect that flies, makes honey, and can sting you.

The word **be** means to exist, to take place, or to go.

    Example: To **be** stung by a **bee** is not fun.

Fill in each of these sentences with the correct **bee** or **be**.

1. You can _____ with this boy.

2. The _____ flew out of the flower.

3. Where can that man _____?

4. I wish for you to _____ happy.

5. The man has three _____ stings!

6. The bear got the honey from the _____ hive.

7. I need to _____ at school early tomorrow morning.

8. I see a _____ on that plant.

9. There are a lot of _____s around today.

10. How would you like to _____ first today?

Challenge: What did the mother bee tell her wild, young son? *(Johnny, be good!)*

Practice: Write a sentence or a joke using each of the above homophones.

_____

_____

          © *Teacher Created Materials, Inc.*

you're   your

The word **you're** is a short way of saying you are.

The word **your** indicates possession, meaning something belongs to you.

Example: **You're** going to be surprised when you see **your** gift.

Fill in each of these sentences with the correct **you're** or **your**.

1. I hear _____ going to see a movie.

2. Is this _____ dog?

3. You can bring _____ apple with you.

4. _____ being funny!

5. I'd like to have _____ picture.

6. Do you think _____ able to come with us?

7. _____ going to have fun at the party.

8. Is he _____ brother?

9. Where do you think _____ going?

10. May I have a piece of _____ candy?

Challenge: What do you say to someone who belongs to himself? *(You're yours.)*

Practice: Write a sentence or a joke using each of the above homophones.

_____

_____

four   for

Four is the number which comes after three.

The word **for** indicates a purpose or destination as in "These are for you" or "He went for a walk."

    Example: These **four** apples are **for** my teacher.

Fill in each of these sentences with the correct **four** or **for**.

1. He has _____ brothers.

2. I am voting _____ the best candidate.

3. I ate _____ pieces of pizza.

4. We only have _____ cookies left.

5. We worked _____ an hour.

6. Run _____ your life!

7. There are _____ chairs at the table.

8. She is looking _____ her cat.

9. These books are _____ the children.

10. Two and two make _____.

Challenge: What has four feet and quacks? *(A quackadile.)*

Practice: Write a sentence or a joke using each of the above homophones.

_____

_____

oar or ore

When you row a boat, you use an **oar** for a paddle.

The word **or** means another choice, as in the phrase you or me.

Ore is a kind of mineral, such as gold, which can be found in a mine under the ground.

> Example: Would you rather have **ore or** an **oar**?

Fill in each of these sentences with the correct **oar**, **or**, or **ore**.

1. The man had an _____ to steer the canoe.

2. Juan _____ Maria will go.

3. There was silver _____ in the mine.

4. Was it the red ball _____ the blue one?

5. Sam put the boat's _____ into the water.

6. The men looked for diamonds in the _____.

7. They hoped to find gold in the _____.

8. I need a new _____ for my boat.

9. Either eat this _____ go hungry.

10. Is the fruit sweet _____ sour?

Challenge: What nickname did they give the miner who wore fancy clothes? *(Ore Nate.)*

Practice: Write a sentence or a joke using each of the above homophones.

_____

_____

LESSON 13 Name _____

one   won

One is the first number after zero and means a single thing.

Won is the past tense of the verb win, meaning to achieve success or victory.

Example: When you've **won** a game, you are number **one**!

Fill in each of these sentences with the correct **one** or **won**.

1. I have _____ sister.

2. Lea _____ the race.

3. Our team _____ the spelling bee.

4. Will you give me _____ of your apples?

5. There is only _____ winner in this contest.

6. The girls _____ first prize.

7. Planet Earth has _____ moon.

8. Who _____ the game last night?

9. _____ boy was standing by the tree.

10. The red team _____ the first race.

Challenge: What can you say about the winner of his first race? *(He won one.)*

Practice: Write a sentence or a joke using each of the above homophones.

_____

_____

there　　　their　　　they're

There refers to a place.

Their shows possession, indicating something belongs to them.

They're is a short way of saying "they are."

    Example: **They're** over **there** playing with **their** toys.

Fill in each of these sentences with the correct **there**, **their**, or **they're**.

1. I see a man over _____ .

2. _____ going to school.

3. Do you have _____ tickets?

4. Our house is white; _____ house is brown.

5. We are going _____ tomorrow.

6. Do you know what time _____ coming?

7. The park is over _____ .

8. Is this _____ dog?

9. _____ coming to visit us today.

10. Please stand _____ quietly.

Challenge: What can you say about people who have finally arrived at a place? *(They're there.)*

Practice: Write a sentence or a joke using each of the above homophones.

_____

_____

maid   made

A **maid** is a girl or unmarried woman. It can also mean a woman servant. (To help you remember, note that the word aid, meaning to help, is in maid.)

The word **made** is the past tense of the verb make, which means to create, get ready, or cause to do something.

Example: Our new **maid** has **made** dinner for us.

Fill in each of these sentences with the correct **maid** or **made**.

1. Father _____ breakfast this morning.

2. I _____ my own lunch.

3. Is the _____ coming today?

4. She was a pretty young _____.

5. The cook _____ the cake.

6. The lady had a _____ to help her.

7. The _____ washed the floor.

8. John _____ a birdhouse.

9. I think you _____ up that story.

10. People with little money don't have _____s.

Challenge: What can you say about a servant who causes you to do something? *(The maid made me.)*

Practice: Write a sentence or a joke using each of the above homophones.

LESSON 16

fined   find

To be **fined** is to have to pay money for breaking a rule or law.

When you **find** something, you discover it.

   Example: It is better to **find** something than to be **fined** for doing something.

Fill in each of these sentences with the correct **fined** or **find**.

   1. The judge _____ the man for speeding.

   2. Please _____ my hat for me.

   3. Would you like to _____ out more about snakes?

   4. In our class we are _____ for talking.

   5. I _____ this book is a good one.

   6. My mother _____ me a dollar for being late.

   7. What did you _____ on the floor?

   8. I hope we _____ that lost dog.

   9. I was _____ for not returning the book.

   10. The man was _____ for breaking the law.

Challenge: What did the judge say to the thief?   *(I find you should be fined.)*

Practice: Write a sentence or a joke using each of the above homophones.

_____

_____

write   right

Write means to make letters or words with an instrument like a pen or pencil.

Right means to be correct or to do what is good. It is also the opposite of wrong and the opposite of the direction left.

Example: Do you **write** with your left or your **right** hand?

Fill in each of these sentences with the correct **write** or **right**.

1. Can you _____ me a letter soon?

2. Turn _____ at the end of the street.

3. He did the _____ thing.

4. You can read and _____.

5. Please _____ on both sides of the paper.

6. Do you have the _____ answer?

7. Show me your _____ arm.

8. I will _____ a list of the things we need.

9. Do you like to _____ stories?

10. I know this is the _____ house.

Challenge: What did the teacher tell the lazy student? *(Write right.)*

Practice: Write a sentence or a joke using each of the above homophones.

_____

_____

no   know

The word **no** is used to express disagreement or refusal. It can also mean not any.

To **know** is to have the facts about or be able to do something.

     Example: I **know** you will have **no** problem with these words!

Fill in each of these sentences with the correct **no** or **know**.

1. _____, I will not go with you.

2. I have _____ apples today.

3. My mother _____s how to cook.

4. An artist must _____ how to draw.

5. There is _____ one home.

6. We _____ that two and two are four.

7. Father told me _____, but I still did it.

8. There will be _____ rain today.

9. I _____ a lot about dogs.

10. Do you _____ how to write your name?

Challenge: What is it when you are aware you did wrong? *(A know no.)*

Practice: Write a sentence or a joke using each of the above homophones.

_____

_____

sum   some

Sum is the total one gets by adding two or more numbers together. It can also mean an amount of money.

Some means a part of or a few.

> Example: **Some** of us got the right **sum** for the addition problem.

Fill in each of these sentences with the correct **sum** or **some**.

1. The _____ of 2 + 3 is 5.

2. _____ girls may go with you.

3. Please drink _____ milk.

4. He paid the _____ of $15 for a new hat.

5. I hope you left _____ pizza for me.

6. He can do easy math _____s in his head.

7. I have a _____ of one dollar.

8. Ask _____ boy to help you.

9. Eat _____ food.

10. What _____ did you get by adding 7 and 8?

Challenge: What do students get when they add two numbers? *(Some sum.)*

Practice: Write a sentence or a joke using each of the above homophones.

_____

_____

LESSON 20

wood   **would**

Wood is the trunk or branches of a tree and can be used for making things.

Would is the past tense of the verb will and indicates choosing to do something.

Example: **Would** you please get some **wood** for the fire?

Fill in each of these sentences with the correct **wood** or **would**.

1. The man bought _____ to build a house.

2. He said that he _____ come.

3. Please put some more _____ on the fire.

4. Is your desk made of _____?

5. He _____ go in spite of our warning.

6. The children _____ play for hours.

7. The man built a table out of _____.

8. _____ you come with me to the store?

9. I _____ like you to be quiet.

10. This _____ came from an oak tree.

Challenge: Try this tongue twister: How much wood would a woodchuck chuck if a woodchuck would chuck wood?

Practice: Write a sentence or a joke using each of the above homophones.

_____

_____

hour   our

An **hour** is a time period of 60 minutes. (Note that the "h" in hour is silent.)

Our shows possession and refers to something belonging to us.

> Example: **Our** train ride took an **hour**.

Fill in each of these sentences with the correct **hour** or **our**.

1. Twenty-four _____s make a day.

2. The news comes on the radio every _____.

3. We need _____ coats today.

4. My breakfast _____ is at seven.

5. This is _____ garden.

6. _____ house is small.

7. It took me an _____ to do the job.

8. Can you come over in an _____?

9. _____ shoes are wet from the rain.

10. Will you help us find _____ dog?

Challenge: What did one grandfather clock say to the other as it chimed? *(Our hour is up.)*

Practice: Write a sentence or a joke using each of the above homophones.

_____

_____

buy   bye   by

Buy means to trade money for something.

Bye is a farewell used when leaving.

By means to be near or beside someone or something.

     Example: They stopped **by** the store to **buy** a gift and then waved **bye** to their friends.

Fill in each of these sentences with the correct **buy**, **bye**, or **by**.

1. She waved good_____ to me as she left.

2. How much would it cost to _____ that book?

3. The garden is _____ the house.

4. I am going to _____ a horse.

5. You can _____ a pencil for 10 cents.

6. "_____," he said as he went away.

7. I don't like having to say good_____ .

8. Would you like to _____ some fruit?

9. The farmer is _____ the barn.

10. Let's go down _____ the river.

Challenge: What did the impatient shopkeeper tell the window shoppers? *(Buy!)*

Practice: Write a sentence or a joke using each of the above homophones.

_____

_____

high   hi

The word **high** means something tall or up above the ground.

Hi is a greeting and is short for hello.

     Example: The people in the **high** tower yelled, "**Hi!**"

Fill in each of these sentences with the correct **high** or **hi**.

1. "_____, Jane," said Joe as he came in.

2. This is a _____ building.

3. The airplane is _____ in the air.

4. Be sure to tell Larry "_____" for me.

5. "_____, how are you?" asked the doctor.

6. The mountain is over 20,000 feet _____.

7. How _____ do you think that window is?

8. "_____ there!   How are you?"

9. Say "_____" to your teacher for me.

10. We climbed _____ into the hills.

Challenge: What do mountain climbers say to each other when they meet? *(High!)*

Practice: Write a sentence or a joke using each of the above homophones.

_____

_____

hole   whole

A **hole** is an opening in something.

Whole means complete or having all the parts.

> Example: Would you rather have a **whole** apple or and an apple with a **hole**?

Fill in each of these sentences with the correct **hole** or **whole**.

1. I have a _____ in my socks.

2. The dog dug a _____ in the ground.

3. He gave her a _____ set of dishes.

4. Swiss cheese has _____s in it.

5. Three thirds make a _____.

6. The dog swallowed the meat _____.

7. If we dig the _____, we can plant the tree.

8. What made this _____ in the ground?

9. I can't believe I ate the _____ thing.

10. He kept me waiting a _____ hour.

Challenge: What is an opening in the ground that has been filled in? *(A whole hole.)*

Practice: Write a sentence or a joke using each of the above homophones.

_____

_____

Mary   marry   merry

Mary is a girl's name.

When people **marry**, they become husband and wife.

Merry is to be jolly or full of fun.

Example: It will be **merry** when **Mary** and Dan finally **marry**.

Fill in each of these sentences with the correct **Mary**, **marry**, or **merry**.

1. Her mother's name is _____.

2. We had a _____ party.

3. Are you coming, _____?

4. He plans to _____ her soon.

5. She has a _____ laugh.

6. The minister will _____ them.

7. I have a sister named _____.

8. We will have a _____ time at the fair.

9. When are you going to _____ him?

10. How many people here are named _____?

Challenge: What did John say to his laughing girlfriend? *(Merry Mary, marry me!)*

Practice: Write a sentence or a joke using each of the above homophones.

_____

_____

see   sea

To **see** means to observe with your eyes or to understand.

A **sea** is a large body of water.

    Example: I sailed over the **sea**, but I didn't **see** any mermaids.

Fill in each of these sentences with the correct **see** or **sea**.

1. You need eyes to _____.

2. Birds fly over the _____.

3. The ship sails on the _____.

4. I _____ a dark cloud in the sky.

5. When I wear my glasses I can _____ better.

6. I like to go to the _____shore.

7. Many fish live in the _____.

8. What do you _____ outside today?

9. Can we go _____ a movie?

10. Parts of the _____ are very deep.

Challenge: What did the toddler say when he went to the ocean? *(See.)*

Practice: Write a sentence or a joke using each of the above homophones.

_____

_____

pear   pair

A **pear** is a kind of fruit.

A **pair** means two of a kind (a pair of shoes) or a thing with two parts that are used together (a pair of scissors).

Example: I need a **pair** of scissors to cut out the picture of a **pear** for my report.

Fill in each of these sentences with the correct **pair** or **pear**.

1. A _____ is good to eat.

2. I have a new _____ of shoes.

3. We have a _____ tree in our yard.

4. The farmer has a _____ of horses.

5. This _____ is sweet and juicy.

6. Do you like my new _____ of pants?

7. Please line up by _____s.

8. Have you ever eaten a _____?

9. We picked _____s off the tree.

10. Here is a _____ of socks.

Challenge: What might you have when you have two fruits? *(A pair of pears.)*

Practice: Write a sentence or a joke using each of the above homophones.

_____

_____

read   red

Read is the past tense of the verb read.

Red is a color.

     Example: His face was **red** with embarrassment because he hadn't **read** the book.

Fill in each of these sentences with the correct **read** or **red**.

1. I _____ that book last year.

2. Sally has _____ hair.

3. Have you _____ this story?

4. He has _____ a lot about dogs.

5. That ball is _____ and white.

6. My favorite color is _____.

7. I have already _____ the paper.

8. I have _____ many books about trees.

9. She was wearing a _____ dress.

10. I like your _____ tie.

Challenge: What is black and white and read all over? *(A newspaper.)*

Practice: Write a sentence or a joke using each of the above homophones.

_____

_____

piece   peace

The word **piece** means a part of something.

Peace is a time when people are not fighting. It also means silence and getting along together.

Example: Would you rather have **peace** in the land or a **piece** of the land?

Fill in each of these sentences with the correct **piece** or **peace**.

1. I am working for world _____.

2. The glass broke into _____s.

3. Please give me a _____ of pie.

4. Could we have _____ in this family?

5. Roberto asked for a _____ of pizza.

6. We enjoy the quiet _____ of the country.

7. If we don't have _____, we will have war.

8. I would like a _____ of that cake.

9. May I have a _____ of your fruit?

10. We hope for _____ on earth.

Challenge: What did the wise man tell his pupils about getting along? *(To have peace, do not speak your piece.)*

Practice: Write a sentence or a joke using each of the above homophones.

_____

_____

plane   plain

A **plane** can refer to an airplane, a flat or level surface, or a carpenter's tool.

Something that is **plain** is simple, clear, ordinary, or easy to understand.

Example: The model **plane** I built was rather **plain**.

Fill in each of these sentences with the correct **plane** or **plain**.

1. The meaning of your letter is _____.

2. The builder used a _____ to even the wood.

3. The man spoke in a _____ way.

4. I am taking a _____ to New York.

5. I like _____, simple things.

6. A flat surface is called a _____.

7. We flew in a _____ across the country.

8. She wore a long, _____ dress.

9. Please tell me that in a _____ way.

10. Have you ever flown in a _____?

Challenge: What do you call an ordinary airplane? *(A plain plane.)*

Practice: Write a sentence or a joke using each of the above homophones.

_____

_____

sun   son

The **sun** is that bright body of light in the sky that is seen during the day.

A **son** is a mother and father's boy child.

Example: My **son** likes to play outdoors when the **sun** is shining.

Fill in each of these sentences with the correct **sun** or **son**.

1. My father has only one _____.

2. I am the oldest _____ in my family.

3. The cat likes to sit in the warm _____.

4. Our _____ is one of many stars.

5. Mary's _____ helped her clean the house.

6. I was burned by the _____.

7. John is Mary's _____.

8. The _____ was bright this morning.

9. Is Tom your _____?

10. I enjoy sitting in the _____.

Challenge: What did the sun name his baby boy? *(Sonny.)*

Practice: Write a sentence or a joke using each of the above homophones.

_____

_____

LESSON 32 Name _____

knew   new

Knew is the past tense of the verb know and refers to having knowledge or expertise at doing something.

New means a thing that has never been before.

> Example: If you already **knew** about it, then it is not **new**.

Fill in each of these sentences with the correct **knew** or **new**.

1. I have a _____ dress.

2. She _____ the right answer.

3. I _____ his house had a red door.

4. We just moved into a _____ house.

5. The class _____ that 2 + 2 = 4.

6. My teacher is _____ to this school.

7. Are your shoes _____?

8. He _____ that was the way to go.

9. We _____ you would come back.

10. The baby is a _____ born.

Challenge: What do you call recent information on a subject? *(A new knew.)*

Practice: Write a sentence or a joke using each of the above homophones.

_____

_____

hear   here

Hear means to listen. (To help you remember, note that the word ear is in hear.)

Here refers to a particular place or time.

      Example: Did you **hear** that our guests are **here**?

Fill in each of these sentences with the correct **hear** or **here**.

1. We live _____.

2. I can _____ my watch tick.

3. Please come _____ for your lesson.

4. You must _____ what he has to say.

5. Where do we go from _____?

6. Do you _____ a noise?

7. Please talk louder; I cannot _____ you.

8. We are _____ by the school.

9. Can you _____ the birds singing?

10. Is everyone _____?

Challenge: What can you say about a person who can listen wherever they are? *(You hear here.)*

Practice: Write a sentence or a joke using each of the above homophones.

_____

_____

clothes   close

Clothes are garments people wear, like a dress or pants.

To **close** is to shut something.

     Example: Please **close** the door of the **clothes** closet.

Fill in each of these sentences with the correct **clothes** or **close**.

1. We need to _____ the window.

2. Mother bought some new _____ for the baby.

3. When you are sleeping, you _____ your eyes.

4. Please _____ the gate.

5. She wore red _____ for the party.

6. All of my _____ are too small!

7. The store will _____ at six today.

8. Will you _____ the car door for me?

9. My sister gave me some of her _____.

10. I like _____ that are clean.

Challenge: Why is the door off the bedroom always shut? *(Because it is a clothes closet.)*

Practice: Write a sentence or a joke using each of the above homophones.

_____

_____

weather   whether

Weather refers to the atmospheric conditions outdoors.

The word **whether** means choosing between things.

      Example: She couldn't decide **whether** she liked hot or cold **weather**.

Fill in each of these sentences with the correct **weather** or **whether**.

  1. He is not certain _____ to work or rest.

  2. The _____ today is windy.

  3. We are having hot _____.

  4. It matters little _____ we go or stay.

  5. In winter the _____ is often very cold.

  6. I'm not sure _____ they will come today.

  7. Who knows _____ it will rain tomorrow.

  8. I like sunny, warm _____.

  9. What is the _____ like in your town?

10. He asked _____ he might leave the room.

Challenge: What do you call a man who can't decide if it will rain? *(A whether weatherman.)*

Practice: Write a sentence or a joke using each of the above homophones.

_____

_____

lead   led

Lead is a metal often used to make pipes. It is also the material used to write with that's inside a pencil.

Led is the past tense of the verb lead and means to show the way or to direct.

Example: He **led** the way to the broken **lead** pipe.

Fill in each of these sentences with the correct **lead** or **led**.

1. These heavy shoes must be made of _____.

2. She _____ me to a special place.

3. This _____ pipe carries water.

4. The man _____ the children across the road.

5. I need to sharpen the _____ in my pencil.

6. That blind man is _____ by his dog.

7. The farmer _____ the children to the farm.

8. There are _____ pipes in my house.

9. My pencil has _____ in the center of it.

10. A woman _____ the singing of the song.

Challenge: What did the pipe say to his slow friend? *(Get the lead out!)*

Practice: Write a sentence or a joke using each of the above homophones.

_____

_____

principal   principle

A **principal** is the head of a school. (To help you remember, note that a principal is a pal.)

A **principle** is an important rule or belief.

 Example: Our **principal** set down a new **principle.**

Fill in each of these sentences with the correct **principal** or **principle**.

1. Our _____ visits our classroom every day.

2. My mother asked to see the school _____.

3. A _____ class rule is to take turns.

4. I make it a _____ to save money each week.

5. The _____ asked how to better our school.

6. I believe in the _____ of telling the truth.

7. Our school _____ is Mrs. Smith.

8. A _____ is the leader of a school.

9. An important _____ is to be fair to others.

10. A good person lives by certain _____s.

Challenge: What do you call a school administrator with high ideals? *(A principled principal.)*

Practice: Write a sentence or a joke using each of the above homophones.

_____

_____

read   reed

To **read** is to get the meaning of writing or print.

A **reed** is a tall grass plant, a part of the mouthpiece in some musical instruments, and a type of wind instrument, like a clarinet.

Example: You need to **read** music to play a **reed** instrument.

Fill in each of these sentences with the correct **read** or **reed**.

1. I like to _____ books.

2. I used a piece of _____ to make music.

3. There are lots of _____s growing by the lake.

4. Will you _____ a story to me?

5. The Indians made baskets out of _____s.

6. Every morning I _____ the newspaper.

7. Did you _____ this story about dogs?

8. How many books do you _____ in a week?

9 A _____ is a kind of plant.

10. The _____ made a soft, high sound.

Challenge: Why is the library like a swamp? *(Because they both have plenty of reeds.)*

Practice: Write a sentence or a joke using each of the above homophones.

_____

_____

sail   sale

To **sail** is to travel on a boat. It also is a large piece of cloth on some ships that catches the wind to make the ship move across the water.

A **sale** is the act of selling, sometimes at a lower cost than usual.

Example: The **sail** for his boat was on **sale**.

Fill in each of these sentences with the correct **sail** or **sale**.

1. That car is for _____.

2. That ship has three _____s.

3. There's no wind so it will be hard to _____.

4. This store is having a _____ on clothes.

5. The _____ of his home made him unhappy.

6. The boys are learning to _____ a boat.

7. My _____ has a hole in it.

8. I bought this table at a _____.

9. The boat's _____ is white.

10. Are these shoes for _____?

Challenge: What do you call a good deal on a sailboat? *(A sail sale.)*

Practice: Write a sentence or a joke using each of the above homophones.

_____

_____

cent　　　　　　　　　sent

A **cent** is a unit of money.

Sent is the past tense of send and means that something has been moved or relayed.

　　Example: I was **sent** to the store and came home with only one **cent** in change.

Fill in each of these sentences with the correct **cent** or **sent**.

1. Mother _____ me to the store for milk.

2. One hundred _____s make up one dollar.

3. The teacher _____ the boy to the office.

4. What can I buy with eight _____s?

5. They _____ the packages last week.

6. I have no money at all — not even one _____.

7. A penny equals one _____.

8. Mary _____ a letter to her sister.

9. Who _____ us these pretty flowers?

10. I need one more _____ to buy this toy.

Challenge: What do you call a penny that was mailed to you?　*(A sent cent.)*

Practice: Write a sentence or a joke using each of the above homophones.

_____

_____

sew   so   sow

To **sew** is to use a needle and thread.

So means in that way, in order that, or to such an extent.

To **sow** is to scatter seeds over the ground or to spread something around.

      Example: One needs to **sew** or **sow** just **so**.

Fill in each of these sentences with the correct **sew**, **so**, or **sow**.

1. Do not walk _____ fast!

2. You can _____ this dress by machine.

3. The farmer will _____ the field with corn.

4. The girl studies _____ that she will do well.

5. Please _____ on this button for me.

6. I need to _____ some grass seed in the yard.

7. He is _____ very kind to me!

8. What kind of seeds will you _____ here?

9. I like to _____ clothes to wear.

10. It was night _____ we went to bed.

Challenge: What did they say about the tailor who wasn't very skilled? *(He sewed so-so.)*

Practice: Write a sentence or a joke using each of the above homophones.

_____

_____

steel   steal

Steel is a metal that is very hard and strong.

To **steal** is to take something that does not belong to you.

Example: Do not **steal** that **steel**.

Fill in each of these sentences with the correct **steel** or **steal**.

1. Robbers _____ money and other things.

2. This sword is made of _____.

3. It is not right to _____.

4. She will _____ some bread to eat.

5. I have a strong _____ shovel.

6. This _____ hammer would be hard to break.

7. Did someone _____ my shoes?

8. The man was sent to jail for _____ing.

9. This knife is made of _____.

10. It's hard to break something made of _____.

Challenge: What does a thief who takes tools do? *(He steals steel.)*

Practice: Write a sentence or a joke using each of the above homophones.

_____

_____

tail   tale

A **tail** is a part of an animal's body that sticks out in back.

A **tale** is a story, often one that is not true.

     Example: Do you know the **tale** about the horse's **tail**?

Fill in each of these sentences with the correct **tail** or **tale**.

1. Rabbits have very short _____s.

2. My dog wags its _____.

3. Father told us a _____ of his boyhood.

4. I enjoy reading folk _____s.

5. A lion has a long _____.

6. The teacher read a _____ to the class.

7. That funny dog is trying to catch its _____.

8. Do you know any _____s about Indians?

9. People do not have _____s.

10. Tell me a _____ about how the world began.

Challenge: What do you call a story about the way an animal got its tail? *(A tail tale.)*

Practice: Write a sentence or a joke using each of the above homophones.

_____

_____

inn   in

An **inn** is a place where travelers can get meals and a room to sleep, a kind of hotel.

In is the opposite of out.

　　　　Example: Please come **in** and see our new **inn**.

Fill in each of these sentences with the correct **inn** or **in**.

1. Please come _____ the house.

2. When we travel, we stay at an _____.

3. I put the candy _____ a box.

4. Hotels have taken the place of many _____s.

5. Let's eat at the downtown _____ today.

6. We live _____ the city.

7. When night came, the man found an _____.

8. The _____ was near the road.

9. The tools are _____ the house.

10. Take your shoes off before you come _____.

Challenge: What's a hotel you can't get out of?　*(An inn.)*

Practice: Write a sentence or a joke using each of the above homophones.

_____

_____

tow   toe

To **tow** is to pull along behind.

A **toe** is one of the five end parts on your foot. It is also the end of a sock or shoe.

   Example: Would you like me to **tow** you by your **toe**?

Fill in each of these sentences with the correct **tow** or **toe**.

1. I have a hole in the _____ of my sock.

2. The baby played with his _____s.

3. The tug boat is _____ing three other boats.

4. The car needs a _____ so it can be fixed.

5. Can you touch your _____ with your elbow?

6. Let's _____ the boat across the lake.

7. John asked the men, "Can you give us a _____?"

8. You have five _____s on each foot.

9. I broke my big _____ when I ran into a rock.

10. Will you help _____ my car into town?

Challenge: What did the cannibal want when his car broke down? *(A toe.)*

Practice: Write a sentence or a joke using each of the above homophones.

_____

_____

week   weak

A **week** is seven consecutive days.

When you are **weak**, you are not strong or not well. It can also mean that something is likely to break.

      Example: He felt **weak** for most of the **week**.

Fill in each of these sentences with the correct **week** or **weak**.

1. We go to school five days out of the _____.

2. He is away most of the _____.

3. The branch of this tree is _____.

4. We are going to spend a _____ at the shore.

5. The man is old and _____.

6. All the heat made him feel _____.

7. Next _____ we will have a spelling test.

8. After running so hard, John felt _____.

9. She is too _____ to be able to stand up.

10. It rained every day last _____.

Challenge: Why did the bridge built in seven days fall down? *(Because it was weak.)*

Practice: Write a sentence or a joke using each of the above homophones.

_____

_____

blew   blue

Blew is the past tense of the verb blow, which refers to being carried by the wind, exhaling air through the mouth, or a sound made by expelling air.

Blue is a color, like the sky on a sunny day. It can also mean unhappy.

    Example: She **blew** up the **blue** balloon.

Fill in each of these sentences with the correct **blew** or **blue**.

1. He was wearing _____ pants.

2. The wind _____ all night long.

3. The children _____ bubbles.

4. My favorite color is _____.

5. The whistle _____ at noon.

6. I felt _____ when I failed the test.

7. The sky is very _____ today.

8. Father _____ up the balloons for us.

9. Please bring me the _____ paper.

10. John _____ on his hands to warm them.

Challenge: What's the wind's favorite color? *(Blue.)*

Practice: Write a sentence or a joke using each of the above homophones.

_____

_____

brake   break

A **brake** is a device used to slow or stop a vehicle from moving as on cars, trains, and bicycles. It also means to reduce speed with such a mechanism.

Break means to cause something to come into pieces or no longer work. It can also mean a change or a pause.

    Example: You would not want to **break** a car, but you need to **brake** a car.

Fill in each of these sentences with the correct **brake** or **break**.

1. The man will _____ the train to stop it.

2. Please push the car's _____ softly.

3. I didn't mean to _____ the window.

4. Be careful or you will _____ that dish.

5. What kind of a _____ is on your bike?

6. There is a _____ in the weather today.

7. The _____s do not work; we're in trouble!

8. Would you like a 10-minute _____?

9. How did you _____ your arm?

10. How do you put on the _____ for this car?

Challenge: Why won't you buy my car? *(It won't brake.)*

Practice: Write a sentence or a joke using each of the above homophones.

_____

_____

creak   creek

A **creak** is a squeaky or raspy sound.

A **creek** is a small stream of water.

     Example: A **creek** makes rushing, bubbling noises, but it does not **creak**.

Fill in each of these sentences with the correct **creak** or **creek**.

1. That _____ runs into a nearby river.

2. That old house _____ed when I walked in it.

3. The door will _____ if I open it.

4. The children played down by the _____.

5. I hear a _____ in the floor over there.

6. Did you catch any fish in the _____?

7. When we came near, we saw a small _____.

8. I was afraid when I heard the loud _____.

9. The water in that _____ is very cold.

10. Do your shoes _____ when you walk?

Challenge: What do old mountains have? *(Creeks.)*

Practice: Write a sentence or a joke using each of the above homophones.

_____

_____

deer   dear

A **deer** is an animal.

A **dear** is someone or something greatly valued or loved. It is also an expression used to show surprise or trouble.

Example: The baby **deer** at the zoo is very **dear**.

Fill in each of these sentences with the correct **deer** or **dear**.

1. His brother was very _____ to him.

2. "Come, my _____," said Mother.

3. Two _____ were eating grass in the woods.

4. My baby sister is a real _____.

5. The _____ ran very fast.

6. The _____ grew a new pair of antlers.

7. Oh _____, where can he be?

8. I want you to meet a _____ friend of mine.

9. The baby _____ lay next to its mother.

10. We have no _____ near our home.

Challenge: What do you call a doe that is loved very much? *(A dear deer.)*

Practice: Write a sentence or a joke using each of the above homophones.

_____

_____

dye   die

Dye is a substance used to color things. It also means to soak items in a coloring solution.

To **die** is to stop living.

   Example: I think I will just **die** if you **dye** your hair green!

Fill in each of these sentences with the correct **dye** or **die**.

1. Did the flowers _____ from cold last night?

2. A good _____ will not lose its color.

3. We bought a bottle of blue _____.

4. When did the man _____?

5. If you cannot get air, you will _____.

6. We are going to _____ eggs for Easter.

7. Let's _____ the cloth green.

8. Plants will _____ if they do not have water.

9. Anything that is alive will finally _____.

10. Could we _____ these shoes a new color?

Challenge: What can you say about real redheads? *(They never dye.)*

Practice: Write a sentence or a joke using each of the above homophones.

_____

_____

fair   fare

When someone is **fair**, he acts to same to everyone. A fair is also a place where people go to have fun and buy things.

A **fare** is money paid to ride on a train, ship, or airplane.

Example: You have to pay a **fare** to get into the **fair**.

Fill in each of these sentences with the correct **fair** or **fare**.

1. Our teacher is very _____.

2. The man is _____ to all people.

3. What is the _____ for this train ride?

4. Our church has a _____ each year.

5. Our airplane _____ was one hundred dollars.

6. She gave the _____ to the driver.

7. Pay the man the _____ for the train ride.

8. We are going to the _____ today.

9. We should be _____ when we play this game.

10. The _____ is one dollar for this trip.

Challenge: What do you call the cost of travel when it is reasonably priced? *(A fair fare.)*

Practice: Write a sentence or a joke using each of the above homophones.

_____

_____

beat   beet

Beat means to hit again and again. It can also mean to win or is a musical rhythm.

A **beet** is a plant with a dark red root that people eat.

     Example: They **beat** the **beet** to make a dye for the cloth.

Fill in each of these sentences with the correct **beat** or **beet**.

  1. The bad man _____ his horse.

  2. We ate _____s last night.

  3. We heard the _____ of a drum.

  4. Our team _____ the other team in the game.

  5. My mother made _____ soup.

  6. The factory makes sugar from _____s.

  7. Do you think we can _____ the other team?

  8. Do you like to eat _____s?

  9. The farmer grows _____s in that field.

10. Please do not _____ that man any more.

Challenge: What is the most tired vegetable? *(A beet.)*

Practice: Write a sentence or a joke using each of the above homophones.

_____

_____

loan   lone

Loan means to let another person borrow something and can also refer to the thing borrowed.

Lone means to be by yourself, without others around, or one of a kind.

Example: If you ask for a **loan** too often, you may find you live a **lone** life.

Fill in each of these sentences with the correct **loan** or **lone**.

1. The _____ traveler was glad to reach home.

2. She asked for the _____ of his pen.

3. He wanted a small _____ to pay his bills.

4. She lived a_____.

5. I will not _____ you any more money.

6. There was a _____ tree in the field.

7. We got a _____ to buy a new car.

8. Please _____ me your ball.

9. I see a _____ bird in the field.

10. A _____ man lives in that house.

Challenge: What do you have when you borrow only one thing at a time? *(A lone loan.)*

Practice: Write a sentence or a joke using each of the above homophones.

_____

_____

road   rowed   rode

A **road** is a street on which vehicles travel.

Rowed is the past tense of the verb row, which means to use oars to make a boat move in water.

Rode is the past tense of the verb ride, which refers to traveling or being carried in a vehicle or on horseback.

Example: Andrew **rode** his bike on the **road**, and he **rowed** his boat on the lake.

Fill in each of these sentences with the correct **road**, **rowed**, or **rode**.

1. We _____ our boat across the lake.

2. Main Street is the name of that _____.

3. Mary _____ in a truck.

4. We _____ 10 miles in the car.

5. He _____ us to the island in his boat.

6. My house is a mile down that _____.

7. Gretchen _____ on a horse.

8. That _____ goes up into the hills.

9. We _____ the boat home.

10. Turn left when you reach the next _____.

Challenge: How did the cowboy get his horse across the river? *(He rowed it.)*

Practice: Write a sentence or a joke using each of the above homophones.

_____

_____

wee   we

Wee means something that is very small.

We refers to a person speaking and one or more others.

Example: **We** saw a **wee** bird.

Fill in each of these sentences with the correct **wee** or **we**.

1. Last night _____ went to sleep late.

2. Look at the _____ bug.

3. You have a _____ spot of food on your face.

4. I think _____ will have a test today.

5. When John arrives, _____ will have a party.

6. I have a _____ hole in my shoe.

7. May I have a _____ bit more to eat?

8. Where shall _____ go today?

9. They lived in a _____, little house.

10. _____ have no more money.

Challenge: What do very small people say about themselves? *(We are wee.)*

Practice: Write a sentence or a joke using each of the above homophones.

_____

_____

it's   **its**

It's is a short way of saying it is or it has.

Its shows possession and means that something belongs to it.

Example: **It's** good that the dog had **its** collar on when it got lost.

Fill in each of these sentences with the correct **it's** or **its**.

1. I think _____ going to rain.

2. The bear moved _____ head.

3. _____ been a while since we read a story.

4. Do you suppose _____ time for bed yet?

5. The tree has lost _____ leaves.

6. The bird built _____ nest in the tree.

7. I know _____ time to go now.

8. Do you think _____ easy to dance?

9. The grass has lost _____ green color.

10. My dog wags _____ tail when he is happy.

Challenge: What might you say when something belongs to something? *(It's its.)*

Practice: Write a sentence or a joke using each of the above homophones.

_____

_____

LESSON 58 Name _____

weigh   way

To **weigh** means to find out how heavy something is.

The word **way** is a path or means of getting from one place to another, a distance, a specific direction, or a person's conduct or manner of behaving.

> Example: What **way** would you use to **weigh** an elephant?

Fill in each of these sentences with the correct **weigh** or **way**.

1. How much do you think you _____?

2. The farmer will _____ the pig.

3. Look this _____.

4. Is this the _____ we should go?

5. I _____ 100 pounds.

6. That child wants his own _____.

7. Let's _____ the fruit.

8. He lived a long _____ from school.

9. What would be the right _____ to do this?

10. Would a dog or a horse _____ more?

Challenge: What do you need to find out how heavy something is? *(A way to weigh.)*

Practice: Write a sentence or a joke using each of the above homophones.

_____

_____

meat   meet

Meat is food or the edible flesh of an animal or fruit. (To help you remember, note that the word eat is in meat.)

To **meet** is to come together.

      Example: We decided to **meet** for some **meat** and drink.

Fill in each of these sentences with the correct **meat** or **meet**.

1. Do you like to eat _____?

2. I would like you to _____ my friend.

3. The man cooked the _____.

4. Mother bought some _____.

5. Please _____ me in the classroom.

6. Would you like to _____ my sister?

7. Where shall we _____ after we eat?

8. We go to the park to _____ our friends.

9. What kind of _____ do you want to eat?

10. Cows produce red _____.

Challenge: What do sandwiches say when they are introduced to each other? *(Nice to meet you.)*

Practice: Write a sentence or a joke using each of the above homophones.

_____

_____

bin   been

A **bin** is a container in which to hold or store things. (To help you remember, note that items are put in a bin.)

The word **been** is the past tense of the verb be, meaning to happen or exist.

     Example: The toys in the **bin** have all **been** played with.

Fill in each of these sentences with the correct **bin** or **been**.

1. The fruit is in the _____.

2. Please put the food in the _____.

3. Do you know where he has _____?

4. She has _____ here all year.

5. We have a _____ of corn over there.

6. Where have you _____?

7. You can put your shoes in that _____.

8. John has _____ late three times this week.

9. Our wood _____ is in back of the house.

10. I have _____ to the store.

Challenge: What do you call a container that holds a lot of items? *(A has bin.)*

Practice: Write a sentence or a joke using each of the above homophones.

_____

_____

shoe   shoo

A **shoe** is a covering for the foot.

Shoo is a word used to frighten animals, insects, or people away.

    Example: I threw my **shoe** at the dog and yelled, "**Shoo!**"

Fill in each of these sentences with the correct **shoe** or **shoo**.

1. Mary put her _____ on her left foot.

2. "Go away! _____ fly!" said the farmer.

3. My new _____s are red.

4. Please _____ the cat off the table.

5. John waved his hand to _____ the birds.

6. I've got my _____ on the wrong foot.

7. My _____ has a hole in it.

8. "_____, children! Go out and play," he said.

9. A loud noise may _____ those birds away.

10. These are _____s I wear for running.

Challenge: What do you have if you send something away with your foot? *(A shoo shoe.)*

Practice: Write a sentence or a joke using each of the above homophones.

_____

_____

herd   heard

A **herd** is a group of animals. It can also mean to form into a group.

Heard is the past tense of the verb hear and means to listen. (To help you remember, note that the word ear is in heard.)

Example: He **heard** the **herd** of horses coming.

Fill in each of these sentences with the correct **herd** or **heard**.

1. Have you _____ the bell ring yet?

2. There is a _____ of elephants over there.

3. Do you see the _____ of cattle in the field?

4. John _____ his mother calling him.

5. The farmer takes care of his _____.

6. Mary thought she _____ a bird singing.

7. The farmer will _____ the cows.

8. When have you _____ this story before?

9. I _____ a loud noise just now.

10. The dog helps the farmer _____ the sheep.

Challenge: What do you call a noisy group of animals? *(A heard herd.)*

Practice: Write a sentence or a joke using each of the above homophones.

_____

_____

LESSON 63 Name _____

tolled   told

The word **tolled** refers to the sound of a bell when it is rung.

Told is the past tense of the verb tell, which means to make known or communicate.

Example: The townspeople were **told** that the bells would be **tolled** at noon.

Fill in each of these sentences with the correct **tolled** or **told**.

1. We were _____ to wait here.

2. I heard the bell being _____.

3. The church bell is _____ each morning.

4. The teacher _____ us a story.

5. Have you been _____ it is your turn?

6. First one bell and then others were _____.

7. I _____ you a true story.

8. The bell on the cow _____ softly.

9. Mother _____ John to come home.

10. When the man died, the bells _____.

Challenge: When did the bells reveal something? *(When they tolled.)*

Practice: Write a sentence or a joke using each of the above homophones.

_____

_____

wear   where

Wear means to have or put on clothes.

The word **where** means in or at what place.

Example: A store is **where** you buy clothes to **wear**.

Fill in each of these sentences with the correct **wear** or **where**.

1. What will you _____ to school today?

2. That is the house _____ he was born.

3. The lady decided to _____ a red dress.

4. _____ warm clothes today because it is cold.

5. _____ do you live?

6. Do you know _____ my shoe is?

7. I don't know which dress to _____ today.

8. I wonder _____ he is now.

9. _____ shall we go after school today?

10. I think I'll _____ my black shoes.

Challenge: What does a girl wonder when she buys a dress? *(Where to wear it.)*

Practice: Write a sentence or a joke using each of the above homophones.

_____

_____

flour   flower

Flour is a fine, powdery substance made by grinding grain, especially wheat.

A **flower** is a plant with a blossom.

Example: The baker put **flour** in the cake and a **flower** on top of it.

Fill in each of these sentences with the correct **flour** or **flower**.

1. That _____ is a beautiful color.

2. We need to buy _____ to make a cake.

3. Please pick some _____s from the yard.

4. Mother put _____ on the meat to brown it.

5. There is a bee near the red _____.

6. I am making cookies with this _____.

7. I like to use whole wheat _____.

8. Look at that pretty blue _____.

9. White _____s would look nice on that dress.

10. You need _____ to cook many things.

Challenge: Why is a bakery like a funeral? *(They both have plenty of flowers.)*

Practice: Write a sentence or a joke using each of the above homophones.

_____

_____

rain   reign   rein

Rain is water that falls from clouds in the sky.

To **reign** means to rule.

A **rein** is a long, narrow strap used to guide or control an animal, such as a horse.

Example: When it started to **rain**, the young prince who had been chosen to **reign** held tightly to his horse's **rein**.

Fill in each of these sentences with the correct **rain**, **reign**, or **rein**.

1. A king _____s over his country.

2. Pull on the right _____ to turn the horse.

3. Do you think it will _____ today?

4. You need to _____ your horse well.

5. The _____ helps the plants to grow.

6. The _____ of a good king helps his country.

7. Use your _____s to control your animal.

8. We can't play outside if the _____ keeps up.

9. The king's _____ was for 20 years.

10. We need more _____ for the plants.

Challenge: What kind of weather did the king have while he was in prison? *(Rain.)*

Practice: Write a sentence or a joke using each of the above homophones.

_____

_____

horse   hoarse

A **horse** is a large, hoofed animal with a long mane and tail.

Hoarse means having a raspy, harsh quality or voice.

Example: Would you rather be a little **horse** or a little **hoarse**?

Fill in each of these sentences with the correct **horse** or **hoarse**.

1. The farmer had a work _____.

2. Your voice sounds _____ today.

3. I like to ride my _____.

4. The _____ pulled the cart around the field.

5. The sound of a frog is _____.

6. I sounded _____ when I got up this morning.

7. There is a _____ in the field.

8. His cold made his voice sound _____.

9. I cannot talk louder because my voice is _____.

10. The farmer named his _____ Speed.

Challenge: What did the doctor say about the small animal who talked too much? *(He's a little hoarse.)*

Practice: Write a sentence or a joke using each of the above homophones.

_____

_____

morn   mourn

Morn is a short way of saying morning, the first part of the day.

To **mourn** is to feel or express sorrow.

Example: This **morn** we gathered to **mourn** the death of our beloved king.

Fill in each of these sentences with the correct **morn** or **mourn**.

1. I heard the birds sing early this _____.

2. They _____ the loss of their president.

3. The people will _____ their leader's death.

4. The first part of the day is the _____.

5. I _____ because I have lost a friend.

6. The _____ is the early part of the day.

7. In the early _____ the birds were singing.

8. It is natural to _____ a lost love.

9. I saw the early light of the _____ing.

10. We all _____ the loss of his father.

Challenge: What is the saddest time of the day? *(The morn.)*

Practice: Write a sentence or a joke using each of the above homophones.

_____

_____

vary   very

Vary means to change or be different.

Very mean much, greatly, or truly.

> Example: The price of goods can **vary** over a period of time **very** much.

Fill in each of these sentences with the correct **vary** or **very**.

1. Stars _____ in how bright they are.

2. The car can go _____ fast.

3. The temperature can _____ from day to day.

4. The cost of food will _____ over time.

5. The sun is _____ hot in the summer.

6. I like this present _____ much.

7. The heat will _____ between day and night.

8. This paper is _____ good.

9. I miss you _____ much.

10. The amount of wind will _____ each day.

Challenge: Why is the weather different from day to day? *(Because it can vary very much.)*

Practice: Write a sentence or a joke using each of the above homophones.

_____

_____

great   grate

Great can mean extremely large or very good.

Grate means to break into pieces or to annoy. It can also mean a set of metal bars over an opening.

Example: After you **grate** things, they aren't so **great** any more.

Fill in each of these sentences with the correct **great** or **grate**.

1. We are having a _____ big party.

2. Please _____ the corn for me.

3. If we _____ the cheese, it will cook faster.

4. She gave me a _____ big smile.

5. Dinosaurs were _____ animals.

6. I need to _____ some carrots for dinner.

7. We had a _____ time at the party.

8. That farmer has a _____ amount of land.

9. Water can pass through that _____.

10. We have a _____ over our fireplace.

Challenge: What is a large opening with bars across it? *(A great grate.)*

Practice: Write a sentence or a joke using each of the above homophones.

_____

_____

threw   through

Threw is the past tense of the verb throw, meaning to hurl.

Through can mean from one side to the other, between the parts of, by way of, or around.

   Example: John **threw** the ball **through** the window.

Fill in each of these sentences with the correct **threw** or **through**.

   1. She read the book all the way _____.

   2. Jim _____ the ball to Joe.

   3. The boys _____ water on us.

   4. We traveled _____ the country.

   5. We _____ the old flowers away.

   6. Will you let the man come _____ the door?

   7. The wind blew _____ the field.

   8. She _____ the old clothes away.

   9. I like the way he _____ that ball.

   10. The man made holes _____ the wood.

Challenge: What did they say about the boy whose ball broke the window? *(He threw it through.)*

Practice: Write a sentence or a joke using each of the above homophones.

_____

_____

need   knead

Need means to require something.

Knead is to mix and work a substance with one's hands or by machine.

Example: I **need** to **knead** the clay before making an object.

Fill in each of these sentences with the correct **need** or **knead**.

1. I _____ some money to go to the show.

2. Machines can be used to _____ the dough.

3. People _____ to have some sleep each night.

4. What do you _____ to do well in school?

5. First, _____ the clay and then form it into a bowl.

6. Will you please _____ this bread dough?

7. I _____ some help with this job.

8. I _____ a new hat.

9. _____ the dough so the bread is lighter.

10. After we _____ the dough, we can shape it.

Challenge: What do you have to do to make dough? *(You need to knead.)*

Practice: Write a sentence or a joke using each of the above homophones.

_____

_____

air   heir

Air is the atmosphere around us or a breeze.

Heir is a person who inherits money, property, or a title or office.

Example: The **heir** to the throne took a walk to get some fresh **air**.

Fill in each of these sentences with the correct **air** or **heir**.

1. The king made his son the _____.

2. Birds fly in the _____.

3. The _____ is clear today.

4. Who will be the _____ to the man's money?

5. They wanted their son to be the _____.

6. Please open the window to let some _____ inside.

7. David is the _____ to his father's property.

8. When the man died, he left no _____.

9. I like to feel the _____ blowing on my face.

10. The _____ is cold early in the morning.

Challenge: When is a man like the weather? *(When he's an heir.)*

Practice: Write a sentence or a joke using each of the above homophones.

_____

_____

add   ad

To **add** means to find the sum of two or more numbers or to combine two or more things together.

Ad is short for advertisement and is a notice to attract attention or business.

Example: When you **add** up the money made, the TV **ad** was very effective.

Fill in each of these sentences with the correct **add** or **ad**.

1. What two numbers _____ up to three?

2. I saw an _____ in the paper for a bike.

3. Let's make an _____ to sell these old toys.

4. Please _____ up these numbers for me.

5. Here is an _____ for a new house.

6. When you _____ two and three, you get five.

7. _____ another stone to the pile.

8. Is that an _____ about dogs for sale?

9. There is an _____ for new clothes.

10. Please _____ more sugar to my glass.

Challenge: What is a good name for a woman who writes commercials? *(Addy.)*

Practice: Write a sentence or a joke using each of the above homophones.

_____

_____

shone   shown

Shone is the past tense of the verb shine, which means to give off light or to excel.

Shown is the past tense of the verb show, referring to having seen or been guided.

Example: Have I **shown** you how the light **shone**?

Fill in each of these sentences with the correct **shone** or **shown**.

1. We were _____ many cars.

2. The light _____ through the window.

3. His face was so clean it _____.

4. Our teacher has _____ us this before.

5. The shoes _____ because they were new.

6. The farmer has _____ the boy his fields.

7. The sun _____ brightly today.

8. Megan was _____ how to do the problem.

9. Has your father _____ you this trick?

10. The moon _____ through the trees.

Challenge: Why couldn't the sun find anything on a cloudy day? *(Because it was never shown.)*

Practice: Write a sentence or a joke using each of the above homophones.

_____

_____

LESSON 76

might   mite

Might means may. It can also mean strength or ability.

A **mite** is tiny animal that lives off others. It can also mean something very small.

     Example: A **mite** does not have much **might**.

Fill in each of these sentences with the correct **might** or **mite**.

1. He _____ have done it already.

2. I can't eat even a _____ more food.

3. We _____ go to the park after we eat.

4. What a _____ that small child is!

5. Do you see any _____s on that plant.

6. John pulled at the door with all his _____.

7. _____ we go home now?

8. _____s are so small they are hard to see.

9. Father used lots of _____ to lift the rock.

10. There are _____s on those flowers.

Challenge: What do you call a very strong, small animal? *(A mighty mite.)*

Practice: Write a sentence or a joke using each of the above homophones.

_____

_____

seam   seem

A **seam** is a line where two edges are joined.

The word **seem** means to look like or appear to be.

Example: The **seam** of my pants does not **seem** to be very strong.

Fill in each of these sentences with the correct **seam** or **seem**.

1. There is a hole in the _____ of my pants.

2. The children _____ to be happy playing.

3. Can you sew up this _____ for me?

4. The boat's _____s must be filled in.

5. Does this room _____ hot to you?

6. There _____s no need to wait any longer.

7. Cut the cloth close to the _____.

8. Where is the _____ in this cloth?

9. It _____s that he's been gone a long time.

10. We all _____ to be here now.

Challenge: Why are clothes never very real? *(Because they have too many seams.)*

Practice: Write a sentence or a joke using each of the above homophones.

_____

_____

LESSON 78 Name _____

side   sighed

A **side** means a surface of an object. It can also mean the right or left part of a person or thing.

Sighed is the past tense of the verb sigh, meaning to let out a long, deep breath or sound.

　　　Example: The wind **sighed** around the **side** of the old house.

Fill in each of these sentences with the correct **side** or **sighed**.

1. She _____ with happiness.

2. The sleepy baby _____.

3. The door is at the _____ of the house.

4. We live on the west _____ of the street.

5. Amy _____ when she learned they had gone.

6. Write on only one _____ of the paper.

7. You have dirt on the left _____ of your face.

8. "Oh dear, where can he be?" _____ Mother.

9. The wind _____ all night long.

10. Line up on the right _____ of the room.

Challenge: What do you call the two sides of a house? *(The inside and the outside.)*

Practice: Write a sentence or a joke using each of the above homophones.

_____

_____

feet   feat

Feet means more than one foot and refers to a unit of measurement or the part of the body.

A **feat** is a great act of courage, strength, or skill.

Example: If you jump six **feet**, that would be a great **feat**.

Fill in each of these sentences with the correct **feet** or **feat**.

1. The man saved the horse, which was a real _____.

2. Most people have two _____.

3. Men who fight fires do great _____s.

4. Do not put your _____ over the line.

5. You can stand on your _____.

6. What a _____ to have come in first.

7. My father is exactly six _____ tall.

8. A yard is three _____ long.

9. People who do great _____s are heroes.

10. I read about a lady who did many _____s.

Challenge: What do you call it when your feet do a great thing? *(A feet feat.)*

Practice: Write a sentence or a joke using each of the above homophones.

_____

_____

night   knight

Night is the time period between sunset and sunrise; it is the opposite of day.

A **knight** is a soldier in olden times who wore armor. It can also mean to grant knighthood to a person.

Example: The brave **knight** disappeared into the **night**.

Fill in each of these sentences with the correct **night** or **knight**.

1. The _____ saved the lady from death.

2. When _____ comes, we go to sleep.

3. Read me a story before the _____ is over.

4. I'll read about the _____s in times long ago.

5. Will Father be home by _____time?

6. The _____ killed the bad man.

7. The king made the man a _____.

8. My mother goes to school at _____.

9. At _____ you can see the stars.

10. The _____ rode a black horse.

Challenge: What time of day are knights most afraid of? *(Nightfall.)*

Practice: Write a sentence or a joke using each of the above homophones.

_____

_____

LESSON 81 Name _____

missed   mist

Missed is the past tense of the verb miss and means that one did not hit, reach, find, get, or meet something or someone.

A **mist** is tiny droplets of water in the atmosphere or on a surface. It is also refers to the fine spray of a liquid, such as perfume.

Example: He got up late and **missed** our walk in the early morning **mist**.

Fill in each of these sentences with the correct **missed** or **mist**.

1. I _____ getting a ride to school.

2. The sun shone through the _____.

3. He _____ the train because he was late.

4. I _____ one word on the test today.

5. I can't see the trees because of the _____.

6. There is a lot of _____ in the air today.

7. I _____ seeing you today.

8. The rain is very fine today, just a light _____.

9. She tried to catch the ball, but _____ it.

10. Drive carefully in the _____ today.

Challenge: What could you say if you weren't hit by the fine rain? *(The mist missed me.)*

Practice: Write a sentence or a joke using each of the above homophones.

_____

_____

reel   real

A **reel** is a spinning device that is used for winding rope, tape, fishing line, or other materials.

When something is **real**, it is true, not made up.

     Example: When Andy was eight, his father gave him a **real** fishing pole and **reel**.

Fill in each of these sentences with the correct **reel** or **real**.

1. I have a new _____ for fishing.

2. Is this dog _____?

3. What is the _____ reason you are late?

4. Please _____ in the rope for me?

5. I bought a new _____.

6. This is the _____ thing.

7. Get your pole and _____, and we'll go fishing.

8. Is that a _____ flower?

9. I need to buy a fishing pole and _____.

10. Is this table made of _____ wood?

Challenge: What can you say about authentic fishing equipment? *(It is real.)*

Practice: Write a sentence or a joke using each of the above homophones.

_____

_____

To complete each of these sentences, choose the correct homophone listed in parentheses.

1. How _____(high/hi) did you climb?

2. You need _____(flour/flower) to bake cookies.

3. I decided to tie- _____(die/dye) my bear.

4. I don't know how to _____(need/knead) dough.

5. My _____(aunt/ ant) is only 20 years old.

6. Every _____(weak/week) I go to the mall.

7. My voice is really getting _____(horse/hoarse).

8. In school, teachers ask for the _____(some/sum) of an equation.

9. I really _____(missed/mist) you.

10. _____(Wood/Would) it be okay to borrow this for a week?

11. The _____(in/inn) we stayed at was very nice.

12. For throwing the spitball, Andrew had to see the _____(principle/principal).

13. _____(Hour/Our) class went to the museum on our field trip.

14. My _____(grate/great) grandmother was a queen.

15. Will you _____(loan/lone) me your jacket?

16. Are you sure that's _____(right/write), Nancy?

17. Every day I like to _____(sea/see) the sunset.

18. How much do you _____(way/weigh)?

19. If you lived in a mansion, you might have a _____(maid/made).

20. We will all _____(morn/mourn) the death of the king.

REVIEW

To complete each of these sentences, choose the correct homophone listed in parentheses.

1. I _____(mite/might) not come to your party.

2. When will I get to _____(meat/meet) her?

3. We tried to be _____(Mary/marry/merry) during our visit.

4. I write with the _____(lead/led) of a pencil.

5. I just _____(knew/new) that would happen.

6. _____(Its/It's) a great honor to meet you.

7. Can you believe I ate a _____(hole/whole) pie.

8. The gold coins _____(shone/shown) very brightly.

9. _____(Here/Hear) ye, a word from your king.

10. You are very _____(fare/fair) when we play games.

11. I am so glad you will help me_____(find/fined) my earrings.

12. My _____(feat/feet) sure do smell.

13. _____(Four/For) little monkeys ate my lunch.

14. Chelsea got something in her _____(eye/I).

15. After school, my brother and I _____(eight/ate) a snack.

16. What a _____(deer/dear) friend you are.

17. That was the best fairy _____(tail/tale) I have heard in a long time.

18. You_____(seem/seam) like a very nice girl.

19. My tastes continue to _____(very/vary).

20. A whole _____(herd/heard) of elephants raced through my kitchen.

Answer Key

Lesson 1, page 6
1. ant
2. ant
3. aunt
4. aunt
5. ant
6. aunt
7. aunt
8. ant
9. ant
10. aunt

Lesson 2, page 7
1. all ready
2. already
3. already
4. all ready
5. already
6. all ready
7. already
8. all ready
9. already
10. all ready

Lesson 3, page 8
1. eight
2. eight
3. ate
4. ate
5. Eight
6. ate
7. ate
8. eight
9. eight
10. ate

Lesson 4, page 9
1. eye
2. I
3. I
4. eye
5. eye
6. I
7. eye
8. I
9. eye
10. I

Lesson 5, page 10
1. bear
2. bare
3. bear
4. bare
5. bare
6. bear
7. bare
8. bare
9. bear
10. bear

Lesson 6, page 11
1. ball
2. bawl
3. ball
4. bawl
5. ball
6. bawl
7. bawl
8. ball
9. ball
10. bawl

Lesson 7, page 12
1. sell
2. sell
3. cell
4. cell
5. sell
6. cell
7. sell
8. sell
9. cell
10. cell

Lesson 8, page 13
1. two
2. too
3. to
4. two
5. too
6. to
7. two
8. to
9. too
10. to

Lesson 9, page 14
1. be
2. bee
3. be
4. be
5. bee
6. bee
7. be
8. bee
9. bee
10. be

Lesson 10, page 15
1. you're
2. your
3. your
4. You're
5. your
6. you're
7. You're
8. your
9. you're
10. your

Lesson 11, page 16
1. four
2. for
3. four
4. four
5. for
6. for
7. four
8. for
9. for
10. four

Lesson 12, page 17
1. oar
2. or
3. ore
4. or
5. oar
6. ore
7. ore
8. oar
9. or
10. or

Lesson 13, page 18
1. one
2. won
3. won
4. one
5. one
6. won
7. one
8. won
9. One
10. won

Lesson 14, page 19
1. there
2. They're
3. their
4. their
5. there
6. they're
7. there
8. their
9. They're
10. there

Answer Key *(cont.)*

Lesson 15, page 20
1. made
2. made
3. maid
4. maid
5. made
6. maid
7. maid
8. made
9. made
10. maid

Lesson 16, page 21
1. fined
2. find
3. find
4. fined
5. find
6. fined
7. find
8. find
9. fined
10. fined

Lesson 17, page 22
1. write
2. right
3. right
4. write
5. write
6. right
7. right
8. write
9. write
10. right

Lesson 18, page 23
1. No
2. no
3. know
4. know
5. no
6. know
7. no
8. no
9. know
10. know

Lesson 19, page 24
1. sum
2. Some
3. some
4. sum
5. some
6. sum
7. sum
8. some
9. some
10. sum

Lesson 20, page 25
1. wood
2. would
3. wood
4. wood
5. would
6. would
7. wood
8. Would
9. would
10. wood

Lesson 21, page 26
1. hour
2. hour
3. our
4. hour
5. our
6. Our
7. hour
8. hour
9. Our
10. our

Lesson 22, page 27
1. Bye
2. buy
3. by
4. buy
5. Buy
6. bye
7. bye
8. Buy
9. by
10. by

Lesson 23, page 28
1. hi
2. high
3. high
4. hi
5. hi
6. high
7. high
8. hi
9. hi
10. high

Lesson 24, page 29
1. hole
2. hole
3. whole
4. hole
5. whole
6. whole
7. hole
8. hole
9. whole
10. whole

Lesson 25, page 30
1. Mary
2. merry
3. Mary
4. marry
5. merry
6. marry
7. Mary
8. merry
9. marry
10. Mary

Lesson 26, page 31
1. see
2. sea
3. sea
4. see
5. see
6. sea
7. sea
8. see
9. see
10. sea

Lesson 27, page 32
1. pear
2. pair
3. pear
4. pair
5. pear
6. pair
7. pair
8. pear
9. pear
10. pair

Lesson 28, page 33
1. read
2. red
3. read
4. read
5. red
6. red
7. read
8. read
9. red
10. red

Answer Key *(cont.)*

Lesson 29, page 34
1. peace
2. piece
3. piece
4. peace
5. piece
6. peace
7. peace
8. piece
9. piece
10. peace

Lesson 30, page 35
1. plain
2. plane
3. plain
4. plane
5. plain
6. plane
7. plane
8. plain
9. plain
10. plane

Lesson 31, page 36
1. son
2. son
3. sun
4. sun
5. son
6. sun
7. son
8. sun
9. son
10. sun

Lesson 32, page 37
1. new
2. knew
3. knew
4. new
5. knew
6. new
7. new
8. knew
9. knew
10. new

Lesson 33, page 38
1. here
2. hear
3. here
4. hear
5. here
6. hear
7. hear
8. here
9. hear
10. here

Lesson 34, page 39
1. close
2. clothes
3. close
4. close
5. clothes
6. clothes
7. close
8. close
9. clothes
10. clothes

Lesson 35, page 40
1. whether
2. weather
3. weather
4. whether
5. weather
6. whether
7. whether
8. weather
9. weather
10. whether

Lesson 36, page 41
1. lead
2. led
3. lead
4. led
5. lead
6. led
7. led
8. lead
9. lead
10. led

Lesson 37, page 42
1. principal
2. principal
3. principle
4. principle
5. principal
6. principle
7. principal
8. principal
9. principle
10. principle

Lesson 38, page 43
1. read
2. reed
3. reed
4. read
5. reed
6. read
7. read
8. read
9. reed
10. reed

Lesson 39, page 44
1. sale
2. sail
3. sail
4. sale
5. sale
6. sail
7. sail
8. sale
9. sail
10. sale

Lesson 40, page 45
1. sent
2. cent
3. sent
4. cent
5. sent
6. cent
7. cent
8. sent
9. sent
10. cent

Lesson 41, page 46
1. so
2. sew
3. sow
4. so
5. sew
6. sow
7. so
8. sow
9. sew
10. so

Lesson 42, page 47
1. steal
2. steel
3. steal
4. steal
5. steel
6. steel
7. steal
8. steal
9. steel
10. steel

Answer Key *(cont.)*

Lesson 43, page 48
1. tail
2. tail
3. tale
4. tale
5. tail
6. tale
7. tail
8. tale
9. tail
10. tale

Lesson 44, page 49
1. in
2. inn
3. in
4. inn
5. inn
6. in
7. inn
8. inn
9. in
10. in

Lesson 45, page 50
1. toe
2. toe
3. tow
4. tow
5. toe
6. tow
7. tow
8. toe
9. toe
10. tow

Lesson 46, page 51
1. week
2. week
3. weak
4. week
5. weak
6. weak
7. week
8. weak
9. weak
10. week

Lesson 47, page 52
1. blue
2. blew
3. blew
4. blue
5. blew
6. blue
7. blue
8. blew
9. blue
10. blew

Lesson 48, page 53
1. brake
2. brake
3. break
4. break
5. brake
6. break
7. brake
8. break
9. break
10. brake

Lesson 49, page 54
1. creek
2. creak
3. creak
4. creek
5. creek
6. creek
7. creek
8. creak
9. creek
10. creak

Lesson 50, page 55
1. dear
2. dear
3. deer
4. dear
5. deer
6. deer
7. dear
8. dear
9. deer
10. deer

Lesson 51, page 56
1. die
2. dye
3. dye
4. die
5. die
6. dye
7. dye
8. die
9. die
10. dye

Lesson 52, page 57
1. fair
2. fair
3. fare
4. fair
5. fare
6. fare
7. fare
8. fair
9. fair
10. fare

Lesson 53, page 58
1. beat
2. beet
3. beat
4. beat
5. beet
6. beet
7. beat
8. beet
9. beet
10. beat

Lesson 54, page 59
1. lone
2. loan
3. loan
4. lone
5. loan
6. lone
7. loan
8. loan
9. lone
10. lone

Lesson 55, page 60
1. rowed
2. road
3. rode
4. rode
5. rowed
6. road
7. rode
8. road
9. rowed
10. road

Lesson 56, page 61
1. we
2. wee
3. wee
4. we
5. we
6. wee
7. wee
8. we
9. wee
10. We

Answer Key *(cont.)*

Lesson 57, page 62
1. it's
2. its
3. It's
4. it's
5. its
6. its
7. it's
8. it's
9. its
10. its

Lesson 58, page 63
1. weigh
2. weigh
3. way
4. way
5. weigh
6. way
7. weigh
8. way
9. way
10. weigh

Lesson 59, page 64
1. meat
2. meet
3. meat
4. meat
5. meet
6. meet
7. meet
8. meet
9. meat
10. meat

Lesson 60, page 65
1. bin
2. bin
3. been
4. been
5. bin
6. been
7. bin
8. been
9. bin
10. been

Lesson 61, page 66
1. shoe
2. shoo
3. shoe
4. shoo
5. shoo
6. shoe
7. shoe
8. Shoo
9. shoo
10. shoe

Lesson 62, page 67
1. heard
2. herd
3. herd
4. heard
5. herd
6. heard
7. herd
8. heard
9. heard
10. herd

Lesson 63, page 68
1. told
2. tolled
3. tolled
4. told
5. told
6. tolled
7. told
8. tolled
9. told
10. tolled

Lesson 64, page 69
1. wear
2. where
3. wear
4. Wear
5. Where
6. where
7. wear
8. where
9. Where
10. wear

Lesson 65, page 70
1. flower
2. flour
3. flower
4. flour
5. flower
6. flour
7. flour
8. flower
9. flower
10. flour

Lesson 66, page 71
1. reign
2. rein
3. rain
4. rein
5. rain
6. reign
7. rein
8. rain
9. reign
10. rain

Lesson 67, page 72
1. horse
2. hoarse
3. horse
4. horse
5. hoarse
6. hoarse
7. horse
8. hoarse
9. hoarse
10. horse

Lesson 68, page 73
1. morn
2. mourn
3. mourn
4. morn
5. mourn
6. morn
7. morn
8. mourn
9. morn
10. mourn

Lesson 69, page 74
1. vary
2. very
3. vary
4. vary
5. very
6. very
7. vary
8. very
9. very
10. vary

Lesson 70, page 75
1. great
2. grate
3. grate
4. great
5. great
6. grate
7. great
8. great
9. grate
10. grate

Answer Key *(cont.)*

Lesson 71, page 76
1. through
2. threw
3. threw
4. through
5. threw
6. through
7. through
8. threw
9. threw
10. through

Lesson 72, page 77
1. need
2. knead
3. need
4. need
5. knead
6. knead
7. need
8. need
9. Knead
10. knead

Lesson 73, page 78
1. heir
2. air
3. air
4. heir
5. heir
6. air
7. heir
8. heir
9. air
10. air

Lesson 74, page 79
1. add
2. ad
3. ad
4. add
5. ad
6. add
7. Add
8. ad
9. ad
10. add

Lesson 75, page 80
1. shown
2. shone
3. shone
4. shown
5. shone
6. shown
7. shone
8. shown
9. shown
10. shone

Lesson 76, page 81
1. might
2. mite
3. might
4. mite
5. mite
6. might
7. Might
8. Mite
9. might
10. mite

Lesson 77, page 82
1. seam
2. seem
3. seam
4. seam
5. seem
6. seem
7. seam
8. seam
9. seem
10. seem

Lesson 78, page 83
1. sighed
2. sighed
3. side
4. side
5. sighed
6. side
7. side
8. sighed
9. sighed
10. side

Lesson 79, page 84
1. feat
2. feet
3. feat
4. feet
5. feet
6. feat
7. feet
8. feet
9. feat
10. feat

Lesson 80, page 85
1. knight
2. night
3. night
4. knight
5. night
6. knight
7. knight
8. night
9. night
10. knight

Lesson 81, page 86
1. missed
2. mist
3. missed
4. missed
5. mist
6. mist
7. missed
8. mist
9. missed
10. mist

Lesson 82, page 87
1. reel
2. real
3. real
4. reel
5. reel
6. real
7. reel
8. real
9. reel
10. real

JEROME LIBRARY
CURRICULUM RESOURCE CENTER
BOWLING GREEN STATE UNIVERSITY
BOWLING GREEN, OHIO 43403

Index

Numbers indicate page numbers.